CROSSDRESSERS:

And Those Who Share Their Lives

Mel expressing his masculine side

Melanie expressing her feminine side

Other Books by Peggy J. Rudd, Ed.D.

MY HUSBAND WEARS MY CLOTHES:
Crossdressing From the Perspective of a Wife

CROSSDRESSING WITH DIGNITY:
The Case for Transcending Gender Lines

LOVE CALENDAR:
The Secrets of Love

PM Publishers will give a discount for special markets including clinicians, universities, book stores, and gender organizations. For information about how these markets or individual consumers can place orders, please write to: Mail Order Department, PM Publishers, P.O. Box 5304, Katy, Texas, 77491-5304. Fax 713-347-8747.

Peggy J. Rudd, Ed.D.

CROSSDRESSERS:
And Those Who Share Their Lives

PM Publishers, Inc.
Katy, Texas

This book is dedicated to my husband, Mel, with deepest love and appreciation. His patience and wisdom have been an inspiration throughout the years.

Books published or distributed by PM Publishers may be purchased for business, and educational use, or for use by gender organizations. For information, please call or write: Marketing Department, PM Publishers, P.O. Box 5304, Katy, TX 77491-5304, (713) 347-6563; Fax (713) 347-8747.

FIRST EDITION
Cover designed by Alfred A. Howell

Library of Congress Cataloging-in-Publication Data

Crossdressers: And Those Who Share Their Lives / Peggy J. Rudd

First printing May, 1995

ISBN 0-9626762-3-3 (cloth)

1. Introduction to crossdressing. 2. Pictures of crossdressers and family members. 3. Crossdressers and their relationships. 4. Religious concerns. 5. Bibliography.

Library of Congress Number 95-068067

CONTENTS

"Looks are so deceptive that people should be done up like food packages with the ingredients clearly labeled."
Helen Hudson

ACKNOWLEDGMENTS

I thank my husband, Mel, for helping with the development of this book, for allowing me to share a part of our lives with readers, and for expanding my understanding of gender issues and concerns. He is always there when I need encouragement, computer expertise, and a love excelled by none.

I would like to express appreciation to the staff of Publishers Press, especially Joel Wyner, for their assistance in technical matters. It's reassuring to know they are never further away than the nearest phone. JoAnn Roberts, of Creative Design Services, reached out a hand of friendship and encouragement as the book neared completion. Such cooperation has turned what could have been a job into a pleasant experience.

A special thanks goes to Dr. Jane Ellen Fairfax for her support. She critiques my material with a very keen eye and always keeps me within appropriate boundaries. I also thank Francine Eileen Murphy, my editor, who believes the topic of crossdressing deserves to be presented accurately and correctly. She guides me as I strive to accomplish this goal. Rev. Kathryn Helms graciously edited the section pertaining to religion, and I was inspired by her input and her life.

I am grateful to my friends who provided pictures and accounts of their experiences. Such contributions will help others find their way through the gender maze. I must not forget the crossdressers and their loved ones who were not able to provide information for this book, but have been a dynamic inspiration throughout the years. You have taught me much about the joys of experiencing life to the fullest.

"The universe is made of stories not atoms."
Muriel Rukeyser

Cover Girl, Melanie, the Georgia Peach

THE GEORGIA PEACH

       The smile is genuine, but life has not always been easy for Melanie. Two marriages have failed with crossdressing figuring into the formula for divorce. Problems are the downfall for some people, but for Melanie difficult life situations have been the catalyst for deeper introspection and an even stronger commitment to self-discovery.

       Professionally, things could not be better for the Georgia Peach. Riding the crest of one of the fastest growing job markets, he has enjoyed the benefits of affluence and the "good life." Career, although exceptionally successful, is not the reason for the smile. Mel/Melanie has found a perfect balance between the masculine and feminine sides. *HE* is as comfortable on the motorcycle as *SHE* is in lace, perfume, and frills. To Melanie real joy comes from being who you are.

Mel says, "Catch me if you can!"

Melanie enjoys expressing her musical side.

Mel is ready for the dance.

....unless Melanie wants to go instead.

Peggy Rudd, Ed.D

A model of masculinity

The model of femininity

Peggy Rudd, Ed.D

With the love of speed.....

....and the love of beauty

Melanie, the balance of masculinity and femininity

MAN ENOUGH TO EXPRESS FEMININITY

"If we are not in harmony with ourselves, how can we possibly be in harmony with anyone else, much less the world we inhabit? We want to lead lives that are whole, without sorrow, anger, fear, stress, and anxiety, yet we continue to define ourselves by these negative outlooks."
Shirley Maclaine

The month of November, 1980, is etched upon my heart forever. I was standing at a crossroads with two paths before me. One path led to the acceptance of my husband's crossdressing. The other led to rejection and denial. My decision represented a turning point; never would life be the same for me. The ultimate changes could have resulted in a destructive force capable of ruining my husband's life as well as my own. This book is about that force, but it is also about a stronger inner ability to follow the wise words of Ann Landers who said, *"Maturity is the ability to live in peace with that which we cannot change."*

THE PATH OF DISCOVERY

That November in 1980 was the time of discovery. First, I discovered my husband's crossdressing and a totally new and unique side of his personality. I also found within me some resistance and negativism which was not pleasant for either of us.

Learning to handle the negative thoughts and resistance taught me that life is patient. When we don't get it right the first time, the experience is repeated, and these repetitions become the patterns of our life. I tried very hard to move forward with finding an inner harmony, a life that was whole, and free from negative emotions. If we were to avoid

11

negative patterns in our relationship, I knew I needed to accept my husband's crossdressing soon. Learning to draw upon the power from within was vital, and both of us knew this power is great enough to supersede any other power. I found harmony and a peace greater than the sorrow, anger, fear, stress, and anxiety associated with the phenomenon of crossdressing.

The path I chose led to acceptance rather than rejection and to happiness rather than sorrow; and led to a new life both for my husband and for me. The primary message of this book is: *Go ahead and deal with crossdressing issues, and the sooner the better.* In the words of Pope John Paul II, "*The worst prison is the closed heart.*" I did not want to spend the rest of my life in that prison, nor do I wish that fate upon my readers.

So it was! The fall of 1980 was the beginning of an adventure. Even as the seasons changed before my eyes, there were major life changes occurring within me. Optimism and a positive attitude were the road maps for greater discovery. The blinders were removed from my eyes so that I could experience a lifestyle which was new and exciting. Very soon I realized that it would be impossible to understand the suffering and conflicts within my husband, and other crossdressers like him, until I fortified my own capacity to love. So the journey which ultimately led me to the role of helper and supporter began in my own heart. There were problems, many of them, but there was also resolution. This book contains many stories of people who are walking the same path. My hope is that the words you read here can serve as guideposts for your own path to discovery.

UNINVITED DILEMMA

"*How adverse or damaging an experience is depends upon how we choose to take it.*"
Richard Zarro

I did not want crossdressing to be an adverse or damaging aspect of my life, but early on I was in need of an attitude adjustment! In order to move in the direction of acceptance, I had to change my thought patterns. The prospect of spending the rest of my life with a crossdresser was not pleasant when perceived in the context of socially acceptable behavior and my own social conditioning. Initially, there was a tendency to reject the dressing and to reject my husband in the same process. I had not known about the crossdressing prior to marriage. Therefore, I thought of this as an unwelcome and uninvited dilemma. Crossdressing was not something chosen or requested; it was imposed upon me. The choice to accept or reject my husband was affected by perceptions, previous thought patterns, and my own present level of knowledge, but I made a deliberate choice to move beyond these factors and into the realm of compassion and empathy. Soon I came to realize that my husband had not chosen crossdressing either, and he also felt pain.

Part of what I had to overcome related to semantics. At that time my husband referred to himself as a transvestite which, unfortunately, was the word of choice for most journalists who sensationalized the stories about persons who rob banks and commit sex crimes while crossdressed. The press made little mention of the thousands of persons who crossdress for emotional satisfaction. Negative journalism set the stage for my own initial misunderstanding. Soon I came to see another side; I came to believe that crossdressers are a group of people who deserve respect and understanding.

Transvestites have been described as persons who wear the clothing of the opposite sex. Kim Elizabeth Stuart, author of THE UNINVITED DILEMMA, does not agree with this definition. *"First, it uses the term opposite 'sex' instead of opposite 'gender'. Gender and sex are often synonymous in person's minds, but gender involves much more than reproductive organs. If all of this seems confusing, it really is not. Gender describes persons and sex is a part of the definition. When transvestites are defined as those persons who wear the clothing of the opposite 'sex' this definition describes the activity and leaves to the imagination the motivation for the activity. In short, it describes a behavioral manifestation of a condition and fails to tell us the nature of the condition. It would be similar to defining apples as something people eat but failing to tell us anything about apples."*

13

In time my knowledge base expanded until there was the realization that crossdressers are men who have a strong feminine component; men who want to experience the feminine side of the personality by wearing women's clothing. Many have said crossdressing allows them to be whole people, in touch with feminine feelings. *Simply stated, the clothes worn by crossdressers are an outward manifestation of an inward feeling.* In some rare examples this may also be a woman who is a crossdresser. She enjoys wearing men's clothes and the clothing helps her experience the masculine side of her personality.

In the past decade I have found some encouraging positive changes in the social perceptions. The trend toward social awareness has reinforced the positive aspects of my own discoveries. Broad change rests exclusively upon the hearts and minds of individuals. While Peter Russell was not talking about gender, his ideas are applicable. *"The transformation of society awaits the transformation of self, and enough selves can tip the balance."* I feel the balance tipping.

LOOKING BEYOND THE CLOTHING

Who are these people we call crossdressers? Their names may change as quickly as their clothing. You may have been introduced to them as Don, Richard, or Harry, but they also like to be called Betty, Susan or Belinda. You have seen them in casual slacks and jackets or in business suits, but it is possible that you may have unknowingly seen them dressed in lace and frills. You might be surprised if you knew what they may wear under their business suits. You will be even more surprised to learn of the depth of emotion felt in their hearts.

It seems evident that a great amount of misunderstanding has resulted because some people look no further than observing the outer activity and fail to look into the hearts and emotions of the crossdressers. People who love crossdressers frequently ask, *"Why is he doing this to me?"* The answer to this question can be found within the motivation, the nature of the individual, and the personal needs. Perhaps the more accurate questions could be asked by the crossdresser. *"Why am I as I am? Why am I so different?"*

With personal growth which comes from reading, interacting with other crossdressers, and introspection, the crossdresser finally finds answers. In time the crossdresser can perceive himself to be gifted rather than handicapped. Once he has come to this realization, the people who love him can perceive the "gift" as well, and move into the belief that everything has worked out for the best. The crossdresser is an individual with a range of emotional expression.

THE IMPACT OF NATIONAL TELEVISION

During recent years, we have learned a little bit more about the phenomenon of crossdressing through national talk shows such as Sally Jessie Raphael, Povich, Springer and Donahue, which have indicated that there may be as many as 10% of the male population who crossdress. These shows have added confusion as well, since the motivation of the participants on the shows have also been varied. The shows may have featured a female impersonator who makes a living in show business or homosexual drag queens who dress like women in order to attract lovers. Sitting next to these persons there may have been a heterosexual crossdresser who dresses for emotional fulfillment.

Even within this sub-group there are differences. Brierley writes about three groups of crossdressers. First, the FETISHISTS are those who dress but make no effort to "feel" like a woman. Second the HETERO-SEXUAL TRANSVESTITES, also known as CROSSDRESSERS, enjoy "passing" as a woman, feeling like a woman, and assuming the social role of a woman from time to time. Third, the TRANSSEXU-ALS, who have an intense desire for sexual reassignment surgery. Ironically, even within groups of crossdressers there is some confusion about personal identity. It is not unusual for a crossdresser to question his own identity or preference. Television has presented the full spectrum and has only given a hint of matters of the heart which motivate crossdressers.

This book will attempt to clear up some of the confusion. It is not about professional impersonators or drag queens. Nor is it about fetishistic crossdressers. Transsexualism will be discussed in an effort to add clarity and help those who may continue to struggle with personal identity. Primarily, this book is about heterosexual crossdressers, many of whom are married and live fairly normal lives. The heterosexual crossdressers you saw on television are the brave ones who are willing to risk their own secret in order to help the world learn to understand and accept this lifestyle. They also want to be certain the world does not confuse them with some other transvestites who may appear on the same television talk show.

National television programmers are anxious to feature stories about crossdressers because of the impact of novelty, but perhaps this is not as novel as once was expected. There are millions of men who feel more fulfilled when they can wear women's clothing and express femininity.

Most people are amazed to read the statistical estimates regarding the number of crossdressers. There are far more than most people expect. You have probably seen them in your own hometown. Who knows who they are? They may be your postman, your doctor, your lawyer, or perhaps your own next door neighbor. Women may be surprised to learn the truth about their own husbands. Many men have told me they sometimes sneak into their wife's lingerie drawer.

THE BIG SECRET

One of the most frequently asked questions is, *"If crossdressing is not wrong, why are most crossdressers so secretive?"* Most are secretive, because they have many fears related to the consequences of having their "big secret" discovered. Some feel guilty because society has placed crossdressers into stereotypes, including the incorrect assumption that all crossdressers are gay. Most crossdressers want to share their life with a woman, and the number of gay males is far less among crossdressers than among the general population. There is a tendency to hide because the behavior of crossdressers may deviate from social norms in the area of gender expression.

One crossdresser, Carla, described efforts to keep the secret from neighbors. Apparently, Carla and her wife live in a nice neighborhood where most people know their neighbors. Carla does go out dressed as a woman, but the disguise is in place before the car leaves the garage. She may be wearing tinted glasses and a baseball hat with a lot of hair stuffed inside. When she is safely out of the neighborhood, off comes the cap and on goes the lipstick. Exit Bill and enter Carla. Believe me, Carla would not go to this much trouble if there were any chance the neighbors would welcome a crossdresser with open arms. Past experience has proven the opposite to be true.

Stories of crossdressers remind me of Superman, or in this case it could also be called "SUPERWOMAN." HE enters a phone booth and, faster than a speeding bullet, SHE makes her exit! I have been told of other cases in which some of the transformations occurred on the freeway after work. This is slightly exaggerated, I think, because most crossdressers I know need a full hour, excellent lighting, a lot of room to add curves with the help of foam padding, and a professionally certified manicurist. All the ingredients of womanhood would definitely NOT fit in a small space. Most of the crossdressers pictured in this book did not step out of a phone booth, but if you are still curious, go ahead and take a second glance as you make your call, and I might suggest you look more closely at the speeding cars on the freeway.

WHY ARE CROSSDRESSERS AFRAID?

"Fear is the dark room where negatives are developed."
E.L. in the AA Grapevine

Is there really cause for fear and paranoia? Many crossdressers seem to think so. Some have experienced rejection by others or they fear such rejection. There is also the fear of detrimental effects upon other family members. There are documented accounts of crossdressers who have lost their jobs when the "secret" got out. Thus, the fears are well grounded, and have prompted other questions such as, *"How will my neighbors react if they find out? What will my children think when they discover this part of me? Will I be criticized, ridiculed, or suffer some other form of verbal abuse? Will people think I am mentally ill? What if they think I am a homosexual? Will my family suffer a loss of social standing? Will I be arrested for using the ladies rest room? "*

Most crossdressers feel society is not ready for such a kaleidoscope of gender expression. A lack of readiness continues to be the catalyst for many fears, but people who are afraid together cause disasters together. The destructive energy can be redirected toward solutions. Many crossdressers have channeled their fear into the formulation of safe environments. Organizations for crossdressers are forming all over the world and have provided the much needed support and security.

WHY DO CROSSDRESSERS FEEL GUILTY?

Fear is not the only emotion keeping crossdressers hidden. Many have feelings of guilt. Initially, crossdressers do not understand the feminine feelings within themselves and tend to mask these feelings with behaviors characterized by macho. Many crossdressers start early in life. Parents sometimes tell them the behavior is wrong, and they believe it. At this early age few have insight into their gender gift, and they hold tenaciously to the masculine qualities and traits expected of them by their parents. Thus, the dominant judge and jury is frequently found from others rather than from within the individual.

Crossdressers may become very confused because they feel a psychological high and an erotic surge of pleasure from wearing feminine clothing. Frequently, they ask themselves the question, *"How could anything that feels so good be so wrong?"* At this point the introspection begins. While looking inward to seek truth they discover their own identity. Many turn to God to find answers. Ideally, the crossdresser will begin to develop a self-awareness and become comfortable with the true self. At some point there is the realization that crossdressing is not a pathological disorder, a sin, or a social wrong. There is no need for guilt.

UNDERSTANDING CROSSDRESSING

Problems for crossdressers and their significant others have been compounded by a lack of tolerance. Crossdressers have had to draw upon common sense rules for problem solving in order to live and exist in society successfully. JoAnn Roberts, owner of Creative Design Services, explained the seriousness of this. *"Nothing seems to disturb society more than when something is discovered to be different from the rest of the so-called 'normal' world. Is it any surprise, then, that behavior society deems appropriate for the opposite sex should cause so much havoc in the personal lives of the crossdresser?"*

This book is written to help clear away some of the misunderstandings that have led to rejection of crossdressers. The crossdressers featured in this book are not gay, mentally ill, perverted, out of touch with reality, or guilty of social wrongdoing or bad behavior.

Ideally, each individual crossdresser will come to understand the nature of these misunderstandings by society. At that point he will learn to accept himself and set individual standards from within, rather than bowing to standards based upon social expectations. Hopefully, by reading the accounts of crossdressers within this book, he will know others have shared the same emotions, the same feelings, and needs. **HE IS NOT ALONE!**

In a broader sense, society needs to be educated. Crossdressers are one of the most misunderstood minorities. For years people have had trouble accepting gender variants. Most critics believe crossdressing is an action of preference rather than an inborn trait. In reality crossdressing is an innate quality of life as basic as being born left-handed or right-handed. Society may accept a left-handed man but has difficulty accepting a man who crossdresses.

IS THERE A CURE?

Many people believe the crossdresser is in need of counseling or psychiatric treatment to find a "cure" for this aberrant behavior. There is no cure. There are only vague theories regarding the etiology of crossdressing. Therefore, the greatest service rendered by counselors and psychiatrists has been helping crossdressers adjust within a hostile social environment. Crossdressers need to learn to accept their own differences, and understand there are many people in our society who feel more comfortable when things progress in a predictable manner. Crossdressing definitely does not fall into the category of the expected norm. Most people do not expect men to put on dresses or express femininity. People say, *"Girls should be girls and boys should be boys,"* but nobody has ever really defined "normal gender expression".

It is time society clarified some critical issues. Do we really want a nation of clones, driven by the need to conform to common-denominator images? Or are we sufficiently mature to accept the challenges and joys related to the diversity of human nature? Can we celebrate the God-given differences which are present within each of us? To take this one step further, do we really want to inhibit full personality expression of the crossdresser?

SEX AND GENDER

When there is more clarity about sex and gender there will be better understanding of crossdressing. Let's start with the basics. Sex is usually determined in the delivery room when the doctor looks at the genitals of the baby and tells the parents they are the proud parents of either a boy or a girl. The primary biological sex roles are assumed from that moment on: boys will impregnate and girls will bear the children. Other behavior, including a person's choice of clothing, is not so clearly defined. Bullough ponders the question of nature versus nurture. *"How much of the behavior associated with one gender or another is biologically programmed and how much is socially and culturally determined? We believe that both forces are at work, but we also believe that not everyone who belongs to the same sex or has the same gender identity is programmed the same way. There are wide variations which, if plotted on a graph, would leave two overlapping bell-shaped curves with males in one hump and females in the other, but with some females more toward the male side than many males are, and vice versa. This does not mean there is confusion about their sexual organs, but that some women are more masculine than others and some men are more feminine. Generally, however, society has tried to ignore this overlap and define behavior in black-and-white terms while in reality there are only shades of gray."*

Bullough questions the need to stay within these boundaries. *"Inevitably, many individuals violate these socially defined norms; crossdressing, in our opinion, represents a symbolic excursion across these boundaries for a wide variety of reasons. Thus, an examination of people who violate traditional gender norms should enrich our understanding of the concept of gender. It is not only important to understand why some individuals crossdress, but why so many do not. What is it that encourages people to stay within the defined gender boundaries?"*

TRENDS TOWARD SOCIAL ACCEPTANCE

Recently we have experienced a trend toward social acceptance for people who crossdress. The trend has been aided by the entertainment world. According to a cover story in USA Today by David Patrick Sterns titled, "Their Style Has Come Into Fashion", people have begun to enjoy seeing performers who explore the masculine and feminine sides of their personalities. While much of what the article says relates to show business, the fact that entertainers are feeling free to cross gender lines, and receive acceptance when they do, seems significant. One point, however, needs to be made clear. The entertainers have a choice of whether or not to dress in the clothing of the opposite gender. Many crossdressers feel they have an innate need to do so.

In the pages which follow we will look into the hearts and faces of a group of people who crossdress. Their stories will show crossdressers to be unique, real, dynamic individuals who are better men because of an interface with femininity. Crossdressers are as worthy of your acceptance even as Cleese, Bakula, or Busch are worthy of your laughter. This book will give you a glimpse of people who dress for personal fulfillment.

There is a growing awareness of gender issues and concerns. The word, "crossdresser", has become widely used and understood due to press and television coverage. Therefore, for the purpose of this book, the term, which was previously written as two words or one hyphenated word, will be written as one word without the hyphen.

Dana and other crossdressers enjoy having their pictures taken. The photographs seem to validate the expression of femininity.

IF A PICTURE IS WORTH A THOUSAND WORDS, THIS BOOK SPEAKS VOLUMES!

THE PICTURE GALLERY

Who are the heterosexual crossdressers? Some of them are race car drivers, broadcast journalists, professional entertainers, business executives, engineers and computer gurus. I know of no occupation that is not represented among them. They are found among all races, creeds, and religious groups, since crossdressers represent the full range of national and international cultures. Some are national political leaders and others are presidents of Fortune Five Hundred corporations. You may sit next to one of them in your church or synagogue or in the board room.

What sets crossdressers apart from other men is their gender gift, the ability to be in touch with the total of humanity; an integration of both masculinity and femininity. Through self-expression and feminine imagery they are able to express a feminine side which is a vital part of their nature.

Crossdressers are more than the sum of their parts. The photographs do not show what is in their hearts, nor do the pictures adequately portray their thoughts and emotions. Each person in this book is a combination of selves: emotional, spiritual, and physical. Many of them have experienced confusion when they realized that all the parts did not match. Compassion is freely given to people who have birth defects, and this is as it should be, but where is the compassion for people who cross gender lines? Society has been less than tolerant. Crossdressers face criticism rather than hugs. Observers should ask these questions. *"What would I do if I had been born this way? Would I be as courageous as the men pictured here?"*

A former race car driver, Linda, has appeared on most national television talk shows.

You may have seen Marie as an entertainer, or you may own one of her albums.

While crossdressers have been compared to Superman who changes roles in a phone booth, you can be sure this beauty had plenty of space, good lighting, and the best makeup to achieve the transformation. It probably did not occur in a phone booth.

For many cossdressers, the first public appearance may
be on Halloween, but the "costume" will probably not
reflect the serious nature of the crossdressing nor the
motivation.

LINDA BUTEN, Board Chair of the International Foundation of Gender Education, based in Waltham, Massachusetts, says, *"Through life as a transvestite, I have encountered a world most men could never know. I have crossed thresholds and unlocked the secrets of both genders. Blessed and thankful, I now reach out to hold the hand of those who seek acceptance. Unquestionably the last ten years of my life have been the most rewarding and enjoyable."*

28

Eve took her most treasured possessions, a skirt and a blouse, when her family fled Marienburg, Germany.

Jami, a computer guru, says, *"As long as I can remember I have had a very large feminine side."*

Brenda Thomas, the founder of HCDA, is frequently the first person crossdressers talk with when they are struggling to come out of the closet.

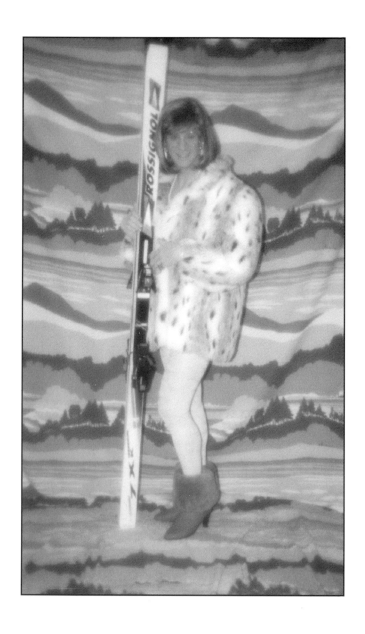

Donna may be seen skiing in the Alps.

...but she no longer equates beautiful clothing with happiness.

ARIADNE KANE

Ariadne Kane is Executive Director of the Outreach Institute of Gender Studies. It is the purpose of OIGS to educate and conduct research in all aspects related to the phenomena of gender. As a social construct, gender phenomena includes a unique and a variable set of attributes. These identify who a person is, what a person does, and how a person acts. It is the basis by which societies and cultures become structured. To achieve these goals OIGS will provide programs, create and implement research, and publish relevant information.

A classy lady and Cissy; one and the same.

Jean teases, *"Do you want to see me walk in five inch pumps?"*

Donahue promised I would meet a girl like Andrea
someday.

Peggy Rudd, Ed.D

FRANCINE EILEEN MURPHY

Francine remembers a long life as a crossdresser. *"From about the age of five I knew that I was different from other boys. When I looked at a girl, I envied her and wished I could be like her. It was at about that age that I first started wearing articles of my mother's or my sister's clothing. I had two older sisters so I had the opportunity but, of course, I had to be very secretive.*

Now at age seventy I still have that strong desire to wear feminine clothing and express my feminine side. I still have that same feminine being within me that wants to live the gender life. And I still feel my life has been enriched because of her."

TERRI LYNN HALL

Terri explains why it is her responsibility to present a favorable image to the world. *"After many years of confusion, I had a great desire to understand myself better. Recently there has been an expansion of my female self, and I am in a phase of discovering my potential. I have never been more calm and sure of what the future holds. The world we experience outside the safe confines of the gender community continues to have many misunderstandings about us and our diversities. There are many who will ridicule, and treat us as less than we really are. My intent is to change those perceptions. By extending a gracious smile and offering to enlighten ignorance, I hope to make people aware that what we are goes deeper than appearance. I would like for them to know that we are all special; those people who stay within their gender lines, and those of us who are blessed with the ability to express both genders. With God's merciful grace the future holds much for me."*

39

Peggy Rudd, Ed.D

Terri Lynn, sitting pretty

VIRGINIA PRINCE, Ph.D

No one person has done more for the world-wide gender community than Virginia Prince. Bullough describes her life and work as follows. "*Though born a male and still a biological male, Prince has for over thirty years lived the life of a woman. Prince was not only able to define herself, but also to organize, publicize, and indoctrinate others about her parameters of transvestism. She organized groups that allowed people to identify themselves and to learn to express in her terms, 'the girl or woman within.' She also established a publishing house that disseminated information around the world; she traveled and made public appearances, and has served as a role model for many transvestites. She has been the dominant voice of transvestism, and it was only in the 1980's, when she was well past the age of retirement, that others challenged her leadership. Even those who disagree with her came to recognize her contributions as the pioneer of the late twentieth-century transvestism.*"

Linda has two chances to be on the cover of SPORTS ILLUSTRATED: as a swim suit model or as a hot rod driver.

Kymberleigh Richards, Publisher and Managing Editor
of CROSS-TALK MAGAZINE

JOANN ROBERTS, PH.D

As a young child, JoAnn Roberts wrote a poem titled, "Busy Hands Are Happy Hands." As an adult she has added real meaning to those words. She is the founder and first Managing Director of Renaissance Educational Association and the co-founder of the Congress of Transgender Organizations. This active leader is the author of several books on crossdressing, most notably "Art & Illusion: A Guide to Crossdressing" and "Coping with Crossdressing." JoAnn publishes other books, magazines and videos for the gender community through Creative Design Services, and is the author of over 200 editorials and essays on community issues, including the original "Bill of Gender Rights." In addition to this she has been the special editor for gender topics in college textbooks, is a frequent speaker at local colleges and universities, and guest on television and radio broadcasts.

TELLING FAMILY AND FRIENDS

"When you love someone you are perceptive of your beloved's relationship to their own life, and not exclusively to your life."
Ken Keys

This book has clearly delineated the thoughts and emotions of crossdressers, their difficult adjustment to being born "different", and the pain they feel as they attempt to live in a world that does not accept or understand them. But what about the people who love them? How does crossdressing affect their lives? Does the wife feel bliss when her husband borrows her pantyhose? The answer to this is, "*Not always, and never without communication, compromise, and love.*"

I have observed many situations in which there should be more sensitivity both from the crossdresser and from those who love him. Friends and family members will fear the negative effects crossdressing may impose upon their lives, and many will believe their boundaries are being violated.

REMEMBERING THE TIME FRAME

Thomas 'a Kempis wrote these words. "*We carefully count other's offenses against us, but we rarely consider what others suffer because of us.*"

It is true! Crossdressers and those who love them spend far too much time thinking about how they have been wronged and far too little time thinking about how others have suffered because of their actions. Let us not

45

forget that each person involved has had moments of feeling he has had to give up too much in the name of crossdressing. There needs to be more concern for loved ones and more mutuality.

It helps when the crossdresser remembers the time-frame of his own self-awareness, provides time for assimilation, and moves away from self long enough to see the concern in the eyes of those people he loves.

Many crossdressers can remember a time when self-image was low. There was little self-tolerance and the need to dress may have been perceived as a handicap or deviation from normal behavior. The crossdresser probably didn't like himself very much but was aware that his need to crossdress could never be purged, at least not for any extended period. Is it any wonder that other people have experienced the same negative emotions when they discover the crossdressing?

Time is vital as family members learn to accept the feminine part of the crossdresser's personality. Think about it! Most crossdressers have known about the very large feminine side for most of their lives, and in many cases it took years for a complete self-adjustment. There were times they may have rejected their own behavior. Getting accustomed to the need to crossdress has been a gradual process occurring over a number of years. When other people suddenly get the news of the crossdressing there is a high level of uneasiness and disbelief. It is too much to comprehend quickly.

David Livingston said, "*I will go anywhere provided it is forward.*" The forward motion in this situation will involve an open mind, flexibility, communication, and the willingness to move forward.

Most people grow up with a clear understanding of what their gender role is supposed to be, and what emotions are acceptable for them. There are also preconceived ideas that dictate which roles are acceptable for other family members. Changing roles or having a loved one step away from expected behaviors is especially difficult for wives. There are more emotional "strings attached" to the husband-wife relationship, and there is almost always a perception of what the "*correct and appropriate*" roles are for husbands.

There is a feeling of security when people stay within their acceptable role descriptions, and it is a shock when they find themselves in a relationship in which there are wide deviations from the norm. The crossdresser must remember to be supportive. The very best way to "*knock the chip off the shoulder*" will be a gentle pat on the back. To say this another way, "*The man who is pulling his own weight never has time to throw it around.*" So, the best way to lead family and friends in the direction of acceptance will be found through patience, love, and understanding. I believe crossdressers will find a higher level of acceptance as they demonstrate the more useful feminine traits such as compassion, tenderness, and nurturing.

HOW AND WHEN TO TELL FAMILY AND FRIENDS

It is a natural thing for crossdessers to want to share all of themselves with those they love, but sometimes the desire is so strong the crossdresser acts impulsively. The desire to tell others must not supersede common sense. As soon as possible he needs to spend some time getting ready to share information about crossdressing. Getting ready includes the following:

1. self-awareness,
2. self-acceptance,
3. a firm knowledge base,
4. literature, and
5. a team of support people.

Telling people about crossdressing can be a frightening experience because there's no guarantee that the results will be positive. The crossdresser must be well fortified with emotional stability and have a clear understanding of who he is. There are issues which must be considered before telling all. As quickly as possible he should deal with the following:

1. Am I sometimes dishonest in my efforts to hide my crossdessing from the people I love? If so, how does this dishonesty affect them?

2. How open-minded are the people I want to tell? For example, how do they feel about other minorities? How well have they processed the knowledge that one of their friends is, in fact, gay? Heterosexual crossdressers are not gay, but people that are tolerant of others who are "different" have the life skills needed to learn to accept crossdressers.

3. Is the love between you strong enough to endure? Have you previously met adversity together and grown stronger in your relationship because of it, or have other problems caused your relationship to be unstable?

4. Will telling them help or hurt the other person?

5. Are my motivations for telling them selfish?

6. What could happen if I tell them?

7. What will happen if I don't tell them?

8. Will I expect them to accept me instantly?

9. Am I emotionally prepared for the awkward period which could follow?

10. Am I prepared to spend more quality time with them as they sort out their feelings and learn more about crossdressing?

GET PREPARED TO SHARE THE NEWS

Shirley Knight has been very successful in telling her friends and family members about her crossdressing, so I have drawn from her wisdom. Shirley believes the crossdresser's attitude about herself is critical. *"If you view your dressing as some dreaded condition that should be cured, your loved one will tend to agree with you and readily share your guilty feelings. When we present crossdressing to others we should share the benefits. We have the opportunity to explore many aspects of life which can never be understood by most men."*

The first family member Shirley told was her sister. It was a pleasant surprise when her response was, *"Is that all there is?"* Later Shirley told her parents and has been delighted with the invitation to visit them crossdressed. Her grandmother's response was classic. She recalled the times she chose to chop wood in overalls. In a quick, dry wit the grandmother replied, *"What's good for the goose is good for the gander!"*

TELLING THE CHILDREN

One of the most difficult questions a crossdresser has to ask is, *"Should I tell the children?"* My answer would be, *"The children are yours, but they are also your wife's, so that makes the decision hers as well. It is very possible that you may not have the same ideas about this, but* ***YOU MUST COME TO AN AGREEMENT BEFORE THE CHILDREN ARE TOLD."***

49

I know some children who know about their father's crossdressing, but there are just as many that have never been told. Many couples wait until the children are grown. It is the decision of the crossdresser to be made jointly with the child's mother. The criteria presented earlier titled, **HOW AND WHEN TO TELL FRIENDS AND FAMILY,** will guide each family in this decision as well, but there are some more specific questions directly related to children's issue and concerns:

1. What is the maturity level of the child?

2. Does the child have other pressing problems that would interfere with acceptance?

3. What about friends that may come over to visit unexpectedly?

4. Can the children keep secrets?

5. Are you prepared to honestly answer your children's questions?

6. Are you willing to step back when the child expresses opposition?

7. Have you reached an agreement with the child's mother about whether or not they should be told?

8. Will you force the issue upon a child that resists your crossdressing?

Shirley beams with pride when talking about her children, a boy and a girl. They were told when both of them were very young. It was the time in their lives when dress up and pretend games were a lot of fun. Everyone enjoyed the games, even when their dad dressed as a woman. Later Shirley explained the emotional impact associated with the dressing.

"There was one major mistake on my part," clarifies Shirley. *"I told one of my daughter's boyfriends without asking her first. This caused some problems for all of us."*

Shirley learned a valuable lesson from this. Children of all ages want their family to appear as "normal" as possible. There is security in staying within expected boundaries. Children are easily embarrassed when the family moves very far from the norm.

All of us make mistakes and have times of bad judgment, but Shirley has done some things right and she gladly shares her secrets of success:

1. Accept yourself first and be proud of who you are.

2. Develop interpersonal skills.

3. Work on being open and honest; first with yourself and later with others.

4. Be emotionally prepared for worse-case scanarios, but hope for the best.

5. Deal with the loneliness which occurs following rejection.

6. Try to emulate the better qualities of both your father and your mother as you develop the total personality.

7. Strive for balance in your life.

To these words of wisdom Shirley adds the following thought, especially for those that have not been as lucky as she has been with family members. *"Many persons within the gender community have been rejected by family and friends and end up closeted, isolated and afraid. Remember that all people may not accept you, but they can like you if you present yourself well. The good news is that society is changing, so crossdressing is not the big negative it once was. Hold on to faith."*

WHEN IT IS NECESSARY TO TELL THE CHILDREN

When Dr. Sheila Kirk became more open with her life as a transgendered person, the reality of telling the children loomed before her. *"I do face the concern of telling the children, for they are certainly going to be surprised for a number of reasons. I will be giving up my medical practice and moving to Boston. Their curiosity will cause them to question the circumstances surrounding the move. This will lead to the declaration of who I am, and I am not sure what I face in that."*

In situations like Sheila's, follow your best instincts, and be very open to the feelings of the children.

TELLING GRANDCHILDREN

If sharing the information about crossdressing is the decision of BOTH parents, we need to realize that grandchildren have parents. It is the responsibility of the parents to tell when the time comes. Our grandchildren were told by THEIR parents when the time was right. The grandsons have attempted to distance themselves, but Misty, our granddaughter, has enjoyed some aspects of her grandfather's crossdressing very much.

I do remember the first evening she spent with Melanie. For the first hour or so the mood was light and fun. Then it happened. Misty crawled up on Melanie's lap and said, *"May I please have my grandfather back?"*

I was pleased to see how fast the feminine clothes went back into the closet. Sensitivity is the rule here! There is such a temptation for crossdressers to claim their rights at the expense of those who love them. They should not succumb to that temptation!

GUIDELINES FOR RELATIONSHIPS

In any relationship there will be problems, but in the relationships involving crossdressing these seem to be more critical. For that reason I have written some helpful guidelines for relationships:

1. Be open and honest.

2. Set your feet firmly in self-confidence; then begin to concentrate more on your loved one's strengths than upon their weaknesses. Concentrate more on your own weaknesses than upon your strengths, and with this type of concentration permit the relationship to grow. Each person has an equal opportunity to become better and, thereby, make the relationship better.

3. Remember that imposing your will upon others will retard the growth process. Replace such actions with cheerfulness. Smiles are the axle grease of the world. Use your smile so that you don't go through life creaking. Turn the frown upside down and "PRESTO CHANGE O!" - you have a smile!

4. Never try to re-make the people you love into something or someone they can not be. To handle yourself use your head. To handle others use your heart.

5. Find love by freely giving it, remembering that what sunshine is to flowers, love is to humanity.

6. Learn to laugh together.

7. Refuse to let problems defeat you. Remember the world is round, and what may seem like the end may actually be the beginning.

8. Take turns at being angry, sad, or upset. Make sure your down moods don't coincide with the down

moods of your loved ones. Some days you may need to say, "*Time out. Today is my turn!*" Honor the wishes of others who make the same request. Remember the words of Confucius. "*The gem cannot be polished without friction nor man without trials.*"

9. Don't forget the value of non-verbal communication. Love held is the seed; love shared is the flower.

10. Some things are best remembered; others are best forgotten. Let your partner help you know which is which. Our eyes are on the front of our head so we can look forward. Past experience should be your guidepost rather than the hitching post.

11. Be the first to forgive, but don't forget to be humble about your ability to forgive. Remember to spell TEAMWORK without the "I".

12. Know that meekness is looking inside, finding the difference between what you are and what you should be, and striving to improve. People who complain about how the ball bounces may be the ones who dropped it.

13. BE the right person rather than SEARCHING for the right person. You can give without loving, but you can not love without giving.

14. Understand that relationships may be made in heaven, but even as it is with toys, some assembling is necessary. While putting it all together watch out for the little things you do or say that may annoy the people you love. Ben Franklin said, "*Small leaks can sink a mighty ship.*"

15. Sometimes forget your own problems for long enough to help your loved ones solve theirs. Kindness is like our daily vitamins. We can each supplement the other's minimum daily requirements.

16. Make home a shelter from problems, not a source of problems. Greet your family with open arms, and say a fond farewell when they leave. Attitudes are contagious, and we want ours to be worth catching.

17. Save some quality time for each other. Kindness is like a boomerang. It always returns.

18. Speak in soft voices especially when there are problems. There is a vast difference between hopeless end and endless hope.

19. Don't spend precious energy trying to figure out whose fault it is when things go wrong. Cooperation involves the whole family.

20. Remember good relationships are more valuable than material gain.

ACCEPTING PEOPLE AS THEY ARE

Perhaps the greatest problem crossdressers face is having a loved one say, "*If you really love me, you would give up dressing.*" The fallacy here is twofold. First of all, crossdressing is not something that can be given up. Also, true love will live even when there are problems. We never expect to like all aspects of a loved one's personality. It is possible to love a person and not like everything about them.

To accept people as they are we must accept ourselves as we are. When we become confident within ourselves, there is less interest in putting others into special molds. Self-confidence is vital for lasting relationships, because there will be greater love for others when we are able to love ourselves. It is when we are dependent upon others for our own sense of value that the relationship may suffer. Personal happiness does not come from others; it comes from within ourselves. Wisconsin's Odd Fellow said it this way: "*It's not so much the world outside, that makes us laugh or cry; It's more the thoughts within our hearts that make life seem worthwhile.*"

Once this confidence is in place we are able to reach out compassionately to others. Compassion is that rare ability to be empathetic when others feel distress. Compassionate people are able to feel the sadness in the other person. Most crossdressers I know have had more than their share of heartache. A family can do much to help ease the pain by showing compassion. Happiness needs to be created and nurtured by all the members of a family. The dividend will be a love returned many fold.

HOW CAN WIVES HELP?

People married to crossdressers have a unique role and have the greatest opportunity to reach out with compassion. How can wives help? First of all, it will be good to move away from the question, "*Why are you doing this to me*?" Being a crossdresser is a real and dynamic life force within the individual. Crossdressers do not choose to be the way they are, and they certainly find no pleasure in forcing it upon others. This fact was substantiated by the research completed in 1990. The data collected for my second book, **CROSSDRESSING WITH DIGNITY,** represented 850 crossdressers from around the world. When all the results were in, the statistical tests showed the greatest fear crossdressers have is the potential harm which could come to loved ones. Crossdressers, as well as their partners, are the real victims of a social injustice, and the thought of imposing this injustice upon the loved ones is a frightening thing for crossdressers to face.

It seems vital for the wife to move from being the victim to being the helper-supporter in a life situation jointly shared. It has been known for centuries, perhaps even from the beginning of time, that adversity can either rip loved ones apart or draw them together. It's always good to move away from "**ME**" and toward "**WE**". Josh Billings said, "*Life consists not in holding good cards, but in playing well those you hold.*" Most wives feel life has dealt them a pretty bad hand, but let's look at the hand which was dealt to the crossdressers. Many times crossdressers have little understanding of the feminine nature within and feel discomfort because of a blurred self-identity. What an adventure it could be if the couple discovered this femininity together.

One of my friends, Rose, tells the story of sharing her femme side with her partner, Valerie. The first response from Valerie was, *"Well, if this is who you are, we will work together to make you the best woman possible."* That statement was just the beginning!

Val helped Rose with makeup, got busy at the sewing machine to create some beautiful new clothes, and helped with wigs. Now Rose has lost about fifty pounds, and is considered one of the best looking "girls" in the Houston Tau Chi Chapter of Tri-Ess, the national organization for heterosexual crossdressers and their families. Valerie is a real living example of what Walter Heily meant when he wrote, *"Happiness is not created by what happens to us, but by our attitudes about each happening."* It isn't our position but our disposition which makes us happy.

Making a marriage or committed relationship work in the context of crossdressing requires efforts by crossdressers as well as the person they love. Each person must do their part to compromise, communicate, and share compassionately with each other. Loved ones can not come to the point of acceptance unless the crossdresser is willing to share openly his feminine feelings and vulnerability.

INTIMACY

Many times the characteristics which caused the initial attraction between a man and a woman cause major differences later. This is the case with many couples involved in crossdressing issues. When the couple meet, and even for several months or years later, the woman is attracted to the more gentle nature the crossdresser possesses. Later it is the feminine side she may wish to purge. When a couple is able to resolve the differences which have divided them, there can be true intimacy.

The word, "intimacy", as used here, has to do with knowing and understanding. For the wife there is the need to know how basic and fundamental these personality traits actually are. It is vital for her to understand the most deep-seated recesses of the heart. Crossdressers should know what brings pain to loved ones and be willing to reach out with compassion. **EVERYONE** in the family has a role in **SHARING COMPASSION**. This is the real meaning of intimacy.

In 1990 Terry Kellogg spoke to the Mental Health Association in Houston, Texas. Kellogg offered these steps for achieving intimacy and for becoming more sensitive to the needs of each other:

1. Ask for what you need.
2. Model how to give it.
3. Allow time.
4. Accept the other person's pace.
5. Have realistic expectations.
6. Give up perfection.
7. Let what is given be enough.
8. Talk, even when it is difficult.
9. Write what you can not say.
10. Send flowers, do lunch, and chat.
11. Respect rituals.
12. Become childlike, but don't stay there.
13. Play together.
14. Touch in a loving way when angry.

15. Don't give kids more attention and nurturing than you give each other.

16. Take risks.

17. Dare to have a different relationship than what you thought a relationship should be.

18. Give up fairy tales.

19. Keep a sense of humor.

THE WISDOM OF BARBARA'S MEMOIR

I believe Barbara Bush said it best. The following quote is a portion of a letter which Barbara wrote to her children. The letter was never mailed, but she included it in her book, BARBARA BUSH: A Memoir.

"For heaven's sake, enjoy life. Don't worry about things that were or things that aren't. Enjoy what you have to the fullest. In all honesty you only have two choices: you can like what you do or you can dislike it. I chose to like my life and what fun I have had. The other choice is no fun, and people do not want to go around a whiner. We can always find people who are worse off than we are, and we don't have to look far. Help them, and forget yourself. I would certainly say, above all, find God. He will come to you if you look. There is absolutely NO down side to sharing life with God."

SISTER ACT

Shirley shares lunch with her sister. All family members know of Shirley's crossdressing including the children, parents, and grandparents. According to Shirley, *"Acceptance from others will follow self-acceptance."*

Mel shares a quiet moment of reflection with his daughter.

Peggy Rudd, Ed.D

Shirley and her mother and grandmother

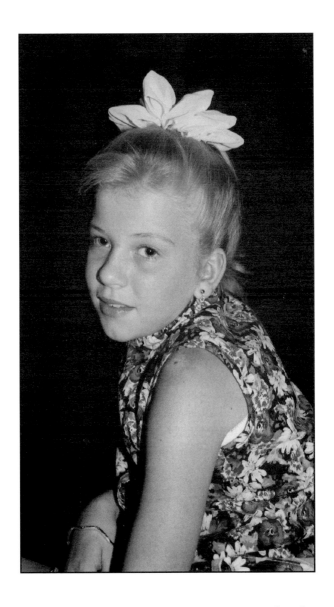

Misty likes to transform her grandfather into a grandmother.

JOAN BRAY

Joan Bray has been a friend to many crossdressers. She assists with makeup, styles hair, and has even been seen at a near-by mall showing one friend how to purchase a new pair of shoes. Later, after a few wobbly steps, the "girl" learned to walk like a lady. Joan's educational programs have helped many crossdressers know which color is best for them and which personality style they project.

The "girls" are frequently invited to Joan's house for good food and fellowship. She even provided a place for the 1994 beauty pageant in Houston. Jean was the winner, with Melanie as the first runner-up. Jean later said, "*I felt like a princess gliding down the beautiful stairs. This was truly a dream come true.*"

MARRIAGE AND THE CROSSDRESSER

"Happiness is inward and not outward; and so it does not depend on what we have, but on what we are.
Henry Van Dyke, as quoted in **LOVE CALENDAR: The Secrets of Love**

Recently I received a letter from Debbie Hahn, who described the diversity of crossdressers and the great range of acceptance levels by their wives and partners. Debbie sees the range of acceptance by wives as extending from intolerant to participatory. I believe she has accurately portrayed the situation within the gender community.

After reading what Debbie had written, I pondered these questions. *"Why is there such a wide range of acceptance levels? What causes the difference? How can a relationship characterized by distrust, fear, and intolerance be led into the bliss experienced by others?"* The answers to these questions will be found when individuals stop depending on other people to "make" them happy and start to look inward for peace and contentment. All aspects of life will then take on a new meaning.

Debbie described her own situation as follows. *"I have told four women of my crossdressing; two wives, one fiancee, and one friend. Each woman was at a different point on the acceptance continuum. The differences are dramatic. I have lived two vastly different marriage experiences. My first wife discovered my dressing by accident and felt it was a perverted behavior. She wanted me cured even if it meant undergoing electric shock treatment. The marriage finally ended, although she had known of the dressing for twelve of the twenty years, and the oldest of our children also knew. I was blackmailed by my wife and her lawyer into an extremely unfair settlement. "*

Blackmail was easy to achieve because Debbie was an officer in the military, and the military is not known for tolerance in such matters. "Taken to the cleaners" does not come close to accurately depicting the settlement as it was described by Debbie.

"On the other end of the spectrum, my new wife, Deborah, is completely tolerant to the point of participation. She believes the wants, needs, and desires that make me a crossdresser also helped me become a caring, loving, and supportive husband. I, better than most, can relate the contrast and extremes on the acceptance continuum, since I have lived them both. "

I have taken the advice of Debbie, and will present the full continuum of acceptance levels. It should be obvious that I do not agree with all the opinions presented here by wives and crossdressers, nor will the readers agree with everything presented. But it is vital to look at the success and failure experienced by couples in the gender community. Reading about the experiences of others, will unlock many of the secrets of success. Look closely at the lives of these people, and learn from their experiences. Remember that what works for one couple may or may not work for others. Then look at your own life objectively and work toward being happy within the context of your own experience.

THE NEGATIVE SIDE OF THE CONTINUUM

Almost all wives and partners of crossdressers have faced the negative aspects of crossdressing; some for only a fleeting moment, but others over a period spanning years. My concern is for the people who continue to harbor negative, destructive thoughts.

It is important to move forward, one way or another, but people should not continue to be miserable. The primary difference between couples who are able to integrate crossdressing into marriage, and those who continue to live in a state of conflict, is the ability to solve problems and handle or dissipate negative factors. Sweeping problems under the rug will not solve them. I always encourage couples to deal with these issues as soon as possible rather than to continue feeling pain. For most problems there is a solution.

A friend, Sandra, agreed to let me write about the problems she now faces in regard to her husband's crossdressing. I do not believe her concerns are much different from the challenges other couples have faced. Solutions will come for Janet and Sandra as they open up to each other honestly and become more sensitive to the needs and feelings of each other.

JANET AND SANDRA

As we talked, Sandra described her life. "*It seems I live in constant fear; fear of the friends and family finding out, fear for job security, fear of the harmful effects the dressing will have upon our sex life, fear that the stress related to crossdressing could lead to alcohol abuse, and of course, the greatest fear of all is that I might someday lose him altogether if he decides to have surgery. Janet and I both feel a lot of tension. I think people are going to notice that he has shaved his body and let his hair and nails grow longer. He might forget to take his fingernail polish off or get caught by the pool with painted toenails.*"

Sandra also feels their lives need new priorities. *"There is the time factor. It seems our whole life is consumed with crossdressing. Other friends have fallen by the wayside in favor of the organization. Even his dressing sessions take a bite out of our lives. He is wanting to spend more and more time dressed up. It gets discouraging, because it seems the more I give in to him, the more he wants. Crossdressing has taken precedent over the other aspects of our lives. He makes promises about 'cutting back', only to break the promises."*

As we talked it seemed evident that Sandra knew what the real problems were. *"If we ever could open up our communication, there are a thousand things I would like to say to him, but I am afraid to openly express my feelings because I can't stand rejection right now."*

I asked Sandra, *"What would you ask Janet if your communication were less restricted?"* In a quick, premeditated manner, Sandra mentioned the following questions:

1. Why did you wait so long to tell me?

2. Does this mean you have other hidden parts of your personality that you plan to spring on me someday?

3. How will you help me when I feel tense about the dressing?

4. How does our sex life fit into the picture?

5. Does making love to you when you are dressed like a woman make me a lesbian?

6. Could you please let me experience your masculine side?

7. Why do you expect me to lie to cover up for you?

8. Why can't you give me more time to learn to accept you?

9. Why can't you understand that on some days I really can't cope with the crossdressing and all our other problems as well?

68

10. Don't you know that crossdressing can't cure all our problems?

11. Could you think about my feelings and my desires?

12. Why can't you express your love with actions and with words?

13. What about our children; is this fair to them?

14. Can we really afford crossdressing?

While the list pretty well sums up Sandra's concerns, the underlying problem went deeper. Sandra felt unimportant and of no value. She felt that her pain, and her desires had been lost in her husband's efforts to "find himself." This is a great lesson. All people need to feel they have value and are valued by the people they love.

Sandra explained it this way. *"I talk, but I am not heard. I ask questions, but they go unanswered. If Janet does give in and restrain from the dressing, he becomes so hard to live with I might even be the person who gives in. He usually misinterprets my encouragement as a higher level of acceptance than I feel."*

My hope is that Sandra will be able to come to a mutual understanding with her husband. Help is out there, especially from the Spouses and Partners Conference on Education held annually for women in committed relationships with crossdressers. In many cities there are support groups for women. But I believe the solution must come primarily from the couple. Both need love and understanding. Mutual concern should be felt and expressed. Janet can do much to make acceptance easier. This will occur when she moves away from herself long enough to see the pain in Sandra's eyes. Sandra should not forget that Janet also feels discomfort. Both people need to reach out with empathy, love, and compassion, as they earnestly try to understand the other person's point of view and needs.

THE POSITIVE SIDE OF THE CONTINUUM

In the search for solutions to the problems faced by couples like Janet and Sandra it sometimes helps to look at couples that have been successful at conflict resolution, communication, and relationship building. There is much to be learned from others. It is important to note that most couples have good days and bad days. I have not met the couple that is able to stay positive, cheerful, and happy all the time. New problems will arise and new challenges will be faced.

JUDY AND LESLIE

Leslie and Judy have worked their way past most of the concerns expressed by Sandra. Leslie says, "*Cross-dressing has enhanced our relationship. We are now experiencing the best years of our lives. I believe the feminine side makes Paul a better person. He no longer gets caught up in the macho trap. How could I not like something that makes him so happy and also makes him a better person? I feel we have a closeness, because there is a dimension to our relationship other couples can not experience. We share so many things, even some of our makeup. He appreciates me more as a woman, because he knows what it takes to look good. His interpersonal skills have been enhanced by his feminine expression. I know Paul's mood is better, and he seems to be more tuned into my feelings.*"

HEATHER AND COLLEEN

Heather and Colleen have successfully integrated crossdressing and the love they feel for each other. They credit communication, trust, and respect, and have used these factors in the process of overcoming the disequilibrium felt by other couples. They believe it is possible to regard crossdressing as a positive rather than a negative force.

In a letter from Colleen she described her marriage as happy and rewarding. *"We have found that an ongoing, honest communication is the most important aspect of our relationship. We never keep any feelings, positive or negative, from one another. Honesty leads to trust. When we were married we vowed to always believe in one another, regardless of the issue or the circumstance."*

I asked Colleen when and how she found out about Heather's crossdressing. *"He did not tell me of his crossdressing before we were married, but he did tell me when the time was right. He wanted to research the subject, and when he did tell me he was armed with literature about heterosexual crossdressing, groups, and sources of support. Because of this many of my initial questions were answered."*

Colleen feels that Heather was extremely patient. *"My husband gave me time to assimilate the information at my own pace. I feel that his patience greatly aided my acceptance. My husband wanted me to share all aspects of his life, and I want that also."*

A very basic part of Heather and Colleen's relationship is respect. They recognize that both of them have unique needs. *"I know Heather wants and needs to express her feminine side. I believe all people have both masculine and feminine components within their*

71

personalities. While the feminine components in Heather are greater than most men, we feel she is a whole person who has found balance in her life. This is precisely the meaning of marriage: to love and share everything."

BRENDA AND ALLISON

Brenda has faced a series of failed marriages, and crossdressing has figured into each failure, but a few years ago the situation turned around. The weeks before telling Allison were a real nightmare. Questions flooded Brenda's mind. *"Do I tell her and risk her walking away like the others did? Will she understand?"*

For Brenda there had been years of repression. Short moments of bliss were always followed by agony. To all crossdressers there comes a time when the secret just has to be made known to those you love. Suppressing the true identity will turn any crossdresser into someone few people can like.

"I knew the time and circumstances had to be right, and they were, because she was a gift from heaven the night I told her. I was prepared for several options, but thank God I did not have to use them." Brenda's formula for happiness as a married crossdresser includes these challenges:

1. Figure out who you are as soon as possible, and communicate who you are as honestly as possible to the people you love.

2. Capture the joys of marriage through mutual sharing.

3. Understand that each life will have sadness, but for every cloud there is a silver lining.

4. Realize that not everyone will love you, but there are people who will.

BARBARA ELLEN AND JOAN

Barbara Ellen credits her wife, Joan, for the happiness they have shared together. Barbara Ellen tells the story of attending their granddaughter's birthday party with Joan all dressed up in Barbara Ellen's clothes. There were many compliments. Barbara Ellen smiled quietly and thought to herself, "*Oh! thank you! The clothing is really mine.*"

If Barbara Ellen ever writes a book, she plans to call it, **MY WIFE WEARS MY CLOTHES**, for she has found much pleasure in sharing clothes with Joan. To Joan belongs the credit for getting Barbara Ellen to attend her first Tri-Ess meeting. "*My feelings were sheer terror,*" explained Barbara Ellen. "*At the meeting door, I actually turned around to leave. Just then the door opened, and Joan gave me a big shove. This was the beginning of a whole new chapter of my life.*"

MADELYN AND KITTY

When Madelyn tells about her relationships there is a special excitement when she talks about Kitty, for Kitty changed Madelyn's life forever. The crossdressers I have met love clothes and love to admire women who take pride in their appearance. Kitty loved beautiful clothes and the two of them shared many happy moments dressing up together. Kitty always dressed to appeal to men, and Madelyn appreciated the effort she put forth to look nice. During one of the dress-up evenings, Kitty came up with the name, Madelyn, and the name stuck.

Madelyn never married Kitty, but based upon her description of the relationship, the love was strong enough to last forever, and crossdressing was a positive factor. Together they shared many aspects of beauty, clothing, makeup, and femininity.

SALLY AND ELLA

Sally believes honesty is the key to making any relationship work, but she does not believe this to be the opposite to intentional lying. This is how Sally remembers the events related to sharing her crossdressing with Ella. As you read this account notice the process which led to total honesty, and note the correlation between honesty and acceptance.

Sally thought she was being honest as she lay shivering with fear confessing for the first time to her wife-to-be that she had always wished to be a girl. It was a big step, and yes, an honest confession, one that was critical to taking the next step to marriage. *"To my astonishment and relief,"* declared Sally, *"she was immediately accepting. When we married I had something I never thought possible, someone who could accept all of me, including that long-hidden side that I thought everyone would reject. I was elated that I didn't have to hide anymore, at least within the confines of drawn household curtains. I didn't dress much, though, sensing a discomfort between us. When I did dress, we tended to avoid much interaction, both pretending nothing was wrong. The honesty had only gone so far."*

As the years went by, Ella would ask Sally how the "problem" was, and Sally would answer, *"It's still there."* Ella was uncomfortable with Sally's dressing, and Sally shared this feeling. *"Thinking we had been open and honest in the beginning, we continued along a path of self-deception, without real, honest communication on the matter for nearly ten years."*

Then one day it ended. Sally's constant pre-occupation with gender conflict, which she had carefully hidden from Ella, became too much. *"I thought I was going to explode. Fortunately I started getting honest again, but this time it was harder, because it went deeper and was shrouded in the agony and stress of a crisis. But instead of going deeper into denial or cutting our own individual paths, we talked and struggled together."*

According to Sally, *"Counseling was tough. Wisely, our counselor insisted we come together. Honesty was hard to find, and the digging was painful. I often didn't like what I found. Honesty was rewarded with gut-wrenching revelation. In one crucial session our counselor asked me, 'So, Sally, you essentially want to continue down this path, and keep Ella around in case it doesn't work out, but perhaps one day you can thank her for a great marriage, and bid her farewell as you go off to become a woman.'"*

That statement was shocking, because for the first time Sally realized exactly what she was doing. She managed a feeble, *"I suppose so."* Ella left the room nauseated. But that was the turning point. Honesty helped this couple realize Sally was really transgendered to the core and she couldn't deny it.

"I also realized that major choices about our future course were ahead. I knew the psychiatrist could not make the decisions for me."

Honesty helped Ella, too. She realized that Sally was as much a part of her husband as the masculine side was. Without Sally the masculine side of the personality would very likely be someone to whom Ella wouldn't have been attracted. Ella began to love Sally. The love replaced a mere tolerance that had previously characterized her feelings. Their honesty brought them through a crisis and into this time of unprecedented closeness.

The story of Sally and Ella is not completely told. Love is a continuous challenge that can be painful and risky to work out. But I'm thankful that at a crucial time in the lives of Sally and Ella they chose to make themselves vulnerable, for it was the vulnerability that helped them find truth.

DONNA AND JULIE

Julie is the exception to the rule that says, *"It is best to tell about the dressing as soon as possible."* Julie's story is very different, for she sees some advantages to being told after the children are grown. According to Julie, *"My husband kept his dressing a secret from me for twenty years. He was afraid of what might happen if I found out."*

Julie could have been very upset about the secret. Many women have been troubled in a similar situation, but she chose to look on the bright side. Julie feels that the adjustment would have been more complicated when the children were young and at home. Donna, Julie's husband, had been borrowing her clothes for years. When Julie and the children were asleep, he would get dressed up, drive to the nearest mall, and walk around to hear the sound of the high heels.

According to Julie, *"Our relationship has deepened over the years because we have learned to integrate communication and compromise in positive ways."*

But Julie admits she is not always positive about crossdressing. *"My emotions can run from being very positive to being extremely negative, but that is okay. Sometimes I am very involved in the community, and other times I back off. Donna has learned to cut back a little from her involvement, and she also knows it is important for Don to be in my life. Discussions on every conceivable aspect of gender and relationships are a big part of our lives, and a part of the formula for our success."*

I have learned many things from Donna and Julie. For one thing they have reinforced the idea that life is not all positive or negative. Many times the long effort to gain understanding reaches the point where the couple can finally feel at ease. They may even laugh and joke about crossdressing, and both the husband and wife feel comfortable. But life situations change, and attitudes change along with them. What is perceived as a source of joy one day can be a problem the next.

Don and Julie have taught me that some ambivalence is okay, and such changes in attitude can even be a source of growth. By watching these two people I have learned that flexibility is indeed a virtue.

JACKIE AND LINDA

Linda has enjoyed marriage to her crossdresser, Jackie, and has moved beyond a mere acceptance into the role as a leader and servant for other women. She has written the following essay which challenges women to hold on to their own identity as they move into the integration of crossdressing into their lives.

WOMAN, WHO ARE YOU?
Reprinted with permission from Linda Peacock

As I talk with women from around the country, and occasionally, to their husbands/partners, it becomes evident that often the woman's self-identity is lost in the struggle of the relationship, and it is lost even more when the relationship is with a gender-influenced man.

Women seem to become so embroiled in trying to find the reason their husband is as he is that they may deny the reality of their husband's gender needs, much as a woman married to an alcoholic or an abuser denies that unfortunate reality. They may lash out at their husbands, accusing them of being someone different, someone the wife does not know. A woman may look into a man's past, trying to find the true, actual cause of his gender dysphoria.

She may consult her spiritual leader and try praying for a "cure," or she may find a sympathetic therapist, who assures her that a "cure" is possible. She may be told that it will take many sessions, at great cost, but the therapist claims to guarantee results. She can set un-realistic boundaries, demanding that the husband stop this dreadful thing immediately, threatening to leave if he doesn't.

A husband may agree to the boundaries, but step over them behind the wife's back, leaving her with a false sense of security and power. I think all this is a mind trip, self-designed to keep a woman from actually facing herself, and who lives inside. As I've said before, if you can't face who you are, how can you ever face who your partner is? If you don't like yourself, how can you like him? If a woman hides from herself, she is hiding from the world, and from life.

I heard a woman minister preach in our church recently, which I found greatly refreshing. Although I didn't particularly like her preaching style, it was im-portant to know that this woman had accepted herself as she was made, and had discovered her worth. She had discovered, too, her work in life, and she defied a society defined by men of the past, and broke through the gender barriers into an ordained ministry.

She realized that gender has no place in seeking what you are meant to do in life, and she pushed ahead to be able to do that work. How truly refreshing!

Societies of old often had a less than complimentary view of womanhood. Only rarely was a woman given the respect she deserved; more often she was used as a sexual chattel, a work horse whose only purpose was to produce children and satisfy a man's sexual appetite. Even women rulers were surrounded by male advisors who directed their rule. Do we read in history about women bishops or women military advisors? There may well have been some, but they must have been a near-nonexistent entity in the pages of history.

Even as recently as the 1950's, didn't we view the perfect woman as June Cleaver, as she happily dusted her living room, and joyfully produced dinner as soon as hubby, Ward, and her well-behaved sons walked in the door at 5 PM? The film industry made comedies of women who were professionals, and they were often shown as "masculine" women. Of course, at the end of the movie, they became far more feminine and were carried off to marriage and motherhood, as all women should be.

We have come a long way in recent years, but I can't help but feel we haven't come far enough. We are too caught up with the past, and what we have been told about our role in life. An example of this is my father's comments of amazement that I can find my way around Little Rock, after only living here ten months. Gee, golly, I guess I should be an "air head" with no sense of direction, always getting lost and having to ask a man how to get where I'm going!

We women are stereotyped, and it is time we break those stereotypes and emerge as the special people we really are. And the one way I can see this happening includes being honest with ourselves, being willing to look inward, accepting who lives inside, learning to like that person, and understanding that we are strong enough to handle the difficulties life may bring us.

We need to learn self-respect, self-honesty, self-love. If we can't give to ourselves, we will never be able to give to others. Self-love is not selfish-love; it is simply caring about yourself, inside and out. It is a step to total health, beginning with your spirit.

Being in any relationship, especially one such as marriage or a similar joining of two people, is always going to enter times of trouble and problems. No one person is perfect, and no two people exactly alike. We stand out by our uniqueness, in physical appearance, in intelligence, in personality, in our humanness. I think we are patterned when we are young to believe that in every committed relationship, there is the "strong one" and the "not-so strong one." Historically, we as women have been the "not-so strong one" in relationships - because men have said that is how we must be!

It is time to break out of this societal prison and accept the freedom of being ourselves. The fact that we are involved with someone who is gender-influenced in no way is a reflection on our uniqueness as a woman. It is not our fault, we didn't cause it, we can't cure it, and we have to make the choice of either living with it or leaving it. If we are healthy in our hearts, and strong in our belief in ourselves, then we can face the issues rationally, and be strong enough to make the decisions we will need to make. If we choose to leave the relationship it won't be easy, but we can adjust when we have the self-strength needed to release the past and anticipate the future.

If we choose to stay in the relationship, we have to reach a place where we can find peace with his dressing. If you are able to look at the entire relationship, the good things about him, and the two of you as a couple, then perhaps you can accept that this man is as human and special as you are. Perhaps, having looked into yourself, and accepted your own uniqueness, you will find it easier to accept his uniqueness. It's worth a shot - do it for you, not him, not me, not society - but find yourself, respect yourself, love yourself.

LIVING THE TRUTH

There is much to be learned from Linda's essay. Remember the Henry Van Dyke quote. "*Happiness is inward and not outward.*" Each person must find his own happiness, and not make happiness dependent on the actions of the one he loves. Face who you are, learn self-respect, self-honesty, and self-love. Crystalize your own identity. Discard the parts you dislike. Develop the better qualities. This is time well spent. Marriage will be much easier with this kind of focus.

The journey to accepting another person or the journey toward embracing a new and different life style must begin from within your own heart. It then moves outward toward others. Carol Beecroft and wife, Norma, have done this. Currently they are organizing a national group for couples. Earlier Carol was the co-founder of Tri-Ess.

Cynthia and Linda Phillips are also involved in outreach. They have opened the doors to their spacious home so frequently it is now affectionately called, THE TRANSVESTITE CASTLE. Cynthia and Linda are always there if a person needs a place to stay, a good meal, or a shoulder to cry on. For the past several years they have been co-chairpersons for the Texas T Party, a national convention for crossdressers and their families.

Communication, trust, and respect are the secrets of a successful marriage for Heather and Colleen.

Barbara Ellen was not ready to attend her first Tri-
Ess meeting until her wife gave her a shove!

A gut-wrenching revelation forced Sally to look deep inside, and what she found there was a turning point for her marriage.

The spacious home of Cynthia and Linda is affectionately called, THE TRANSVESTITE CASTLE.

Carol and Norma have formed a national organization for couples in the gender community.

THE CROSSDRESSER AND RELIGION

If God is small enough for us to understand, He isn't big enough for us to worship.

Most crossdressers and those who love them have experienced the introspection described within this book. The gender community is desperately searching for its place in the world. Soon after discovering that my husband was a crossdresser, I began to sort out the moral and religious concerns. There was much I did not understand. Although, in most cases, I was capable of knowing what is right for my life, the lines seemed to be blurred in regard to crossdressing issues. How could I sort out right from wrong within the gender community when I could not understand how religion fits into the picture?

I began my quest for truth within the Christian faith, but I am aware that many crossdressers come from other faiths or share no religious experience. Rev. Kathryn Helms explains some interpretations. *"Because religion is concerned with all aspects of human life, it has an interest in cross gender behavior as well. Religion may manifest itself through cross gender behavior, recognize but not approve, or reject such behavior as demonic."*

Helms continued by providing specific examples. *"For religions which view the universe from a monistic view point, cross gender behavior is but an affirmation of the essential continuity of all life and a natural expression of the spectrum of life. Religions such as animist, pantheist, and Hindu/Buddhist all embrace a monistic view of life. But religions which have a strongly transcendent view of the separation of the divine and creation such as Christianity, Judaism, and Islam offer no formal place for cross gender behavior in their rituals."*

My husband is a Christian, and I knew he would not turn away from God deliberately nor would he forsake the truths that had been taught by the church. For most of his life the church had established guidelines for proper behavior, actions, and even thoughts. As a couple we had stayed within these parameters, but in the matter of crossdressing I felt a disequilibrium.

Examination of my own heart was very intense. To correctly describe my life, the word CONSERVATIVE would need to be spelled out with all capital letters. My whole life had been predictable, religious, and somewhat rigid. I faced three challenges:

1. to discover the will of God for my life,

2. to accept my husband as a crossdresser, and

3. to make our marriage work within the context of crossdressing.

SEEKING GUIDANCE FROM THE BIBLE

My life long need to discover Biblical truths led me directly to Deuteronomy 22:5. *"A woman shall not wear anything that pertains to a man, nor shall a man put on a woman's garment; for whosoever does these things is an abomination to the Lord your God."* It seemed to me nothing could be clearer than the words of this Bible verse. However, closer study revealed that this passage had been taken out of context, and the verse had to do with the way people were worshiping during Bible times. According to Bible scholar, David Payne, *"There is good reason to suppose that the law of verse 5 is not concerned with mild sexual aberration associated with transvestism, but is a repudiation of certain pagan practices of that era; so this verse is no more a fashion guide for today than it is the law about tassels in verse 12."*

Further study revealed that the dress of men and women during Bible times differed in detail rather than in kind, although no interchange was permitted, nor was mixing of materials permitted. (Leviticus 19:19) The fabric used for women's clothing was made to be modest. (I Tim.2:9) The word "modest" was one of the first signals to me that we are living in a different time and place, for women have no longer continued to wear "modest", drab clothing, and there are different cultural expectations. In time I came to believe this scripture has more to do with the rituals of religion centuries ago than it has to do with crossdressers in today's world.

I have found no reference in the Bible which says it is wrong for men to dress in feminine clothing as an expression of inner feelings, nor can I find any passage which condemns the joy or subsequent feelings of happiness. The most applicable message of the Bible speaks of love, and this is true both for the New Testament and the Old Testament. Love has the power to supersede uncertainty, prejudice, and the disequilibrium which crossdressers may experience. Love also does much to heal the pain felt by those who love them. Here are some key scriptures which reinforce this truth.

"You shall love your neighbor as thyself." (Leviticus 19:18)

"This I command you, to love one another. If the world hates you, know that it has hated me before it hated you." (John 15: 17-18)

"Hold fast to love and justice." (Hosea 11:4)

I heard the message of the Bible clearly saying to me, *"Love each other. What is in the heart counts more than what covers the body."* Shirley Maclaine echoed the thought. *"The purpose of life is to learn love. As we*

89

evolve we learn to love and to be loved." When we make love the controlling force of our lives, we will be able to:

1. outgrow selfishness,
2. be sensitive to the needs of loved ones,
3. accept people as they are, whether or not we understand them,
4. maximize the time spent with family,
5. think of effect before acting or speaking,
6. learn to empathize, and
7. be able to forgive self and others.

If each person masters these seven practices of love, the specific social wrongs listed below may have ready solutions. I am not God, so it is impossible for me to determine what is inappropriate for another person's life, but I will list some "gray areas" which are frequently found in the gender community. First, let me state my position about the community in general. *I am a champion of crossdressers, and I believe collectively they are the most outstanding people I have met.* There are, however, some things which alarm me, and these must be addressed. Hopefully, we can more away from the matter of how people dress and focus our energy in the direction of the real issues. **These social wrongs have an application within most religions.**

VANITY

"A person all wrapped up in himself makes a pretty small package."
Joseph Cossman

Find a hundred crossdressers in one place and you will find two hundred mirrors, and most of the mirrors will be visible during any given time. Is this statistical data? No, it is a tongue-in-cheek observation, but it addresses the issue of vanity which has the potential of affecting life negatively. When the focus is upon personal looks and accomplishment, rather than upon the feelings and needs of others, this can be harmful. Sometimes I glance at my own husband, mirror in hand, and remember the words of Louisa M. Alcott who wrote, *"Despite her small vanities, Margaret had a sweet nature."* The real challenge is to be pretty, to be sweet, and to be aware of good grooming while being careful to present a good image of femininity. At the same time maintain a positive attitude about self and others. As the psalmist said, *"Turn my eyes from looking at vanities, and give me life in thy ways."* God's way includes concern for others.

Love must be the guiding force of our lives. *"With all lowliness, and meekness, with patience, forbearing with each other in love, eager to maintain unity and the bond of peace."* (Ephesians 4: 2)

SELFISHNESS

Unfortunately there is a lot of self-indulgence in the gender community. Sometimes the gratification of selfish desires supersedes the concerns for others. We need to think about the harm that may come to the special people in our lives. The harm may be expressed emotionally, financially, and perhaps even spiritually. Crossdressers who are able to have successful interaction with others are able to move beyond the capricious, selfish tendencies, and look into the eyes of those people who share their lives. Samuel Johnson once said, *"WANT makes almost every man selfish."* Crossdressers do have many unfulfilled dreams and desires, but how much better it is when the search for fulfillment also includes a concern for others. Caring too much for self and not enough for others can be very damaging, and I believe this is potentially sinful. *"Do nothing from selfishness or conceit, but in humility. Count others better than yourself."* (Philippians 2:3)

THE "TRAMP" FACTOR

A few years ago we listened to a song titled, THE WOMAN IS A TRAMP. We took the theme of the song lightly, but one of my first concerns after learning of my husband's crossdressing had to do with the image many crossdressers portrayed. Did they really want to be tramps? I came to believe that for some crossdressers this image is an effort to expand the boundaries of life to the maximum. It represents the desire to touch and feel all aspects of femininity; the glamour, beauty, and sensuality. On the other hand, some expressions of this image do not seem consistent with morality, since such an image is almost a devaluation of femininity. I can't determine whether or not this is a sin, and it may not be, but I believe people of faith should present themselves as honorable. Image does much to speak for character.

What is the "tramp" factor? This is the desire to present an image that is not ladylike. Many crossdressers have felt a need to express this side of their personality. I have pondered these desires and have a theory. If there is a relationship between crossdressing and sex, we have to look at what the sexual "triggers" are. Some research is beginning to show a relationship between a crossdresser's early sexual attractions and their projected image as a woman. The appeal of a sexy show girl can not be denied. Perhaps the word of advice would be to express this side of your personality, if the need exists, but use discretion. In most cases this is not a good image when you are still trying to teach your wife the joys of being married to a crossdresser or convince society that the gender community has credibility.

I should hasten to add, however, that some wives or girlfriends may actually enjoy the beauty of sexy lingerie and risque behavior, specifically women that are into what psychiatrists call the prostitute-Madonna complex. In this scenario, the image of being a good wife and mother is important, but at the same time there is a feeling of being lustful or seductive. Recently I have met a number of couples who enjoy this image together. I think what a couple experiences in the privacy of their own home is their business, but open public expressions of the "tramp" may not be good.

DISHONESTY

"Behold thou desirest truth in the inward being; therefore teach me wisdom in my secret heart." Psalms 51: 6

Oh! How difficult it is to be honest when you are born a male with a very large capacity to experience femininity! How do you explain the chapter meetings to a wife who does not know her husband is a crossdresser? How do you explain the locked closet which your children can not open? Who are these friends you just happen to see when you are out with the family? How do you justify hiding the feminine side or hiding behind a macho front? All of life must be a masquerade.

On the ANGELA SHOW, a regional television talk show filmed in New Orleans, Michelle was asked if she ever felt like an actor when dressed like a woman. Her reply was very insightful. *"Yes, we are all consummate actors, especially when dressed as men."*

What is the answer? How do crossdressers keep the secret and still stay honest? I do not know, but I do know what the Bible says about truth. I will give you the scriptures and leave the interpretation to you. *"Lead me in thy truth, and teach me, for thou art the God of my salvation."* (Psalms 25: 5) *"Those who worship Him, must worship Him in spirit and in truth."* (John 4: 24) *"And you will know the truth, and the truth shall make you free."* (John 8: 32)

These scriptures describe truth as the best teacher. All people can overcome problem areas if honesty is the motivating force. Life will be better for all people concerned when truth is met face to face. Then the true nature of crossdressers will be visible, a community of gifted individuals with rare insight and ability.

IDOLATRY AND LOVE OF POWER

"What each of us needs to do is substitute the love of power with the power of love."
From **LOVE CALENDAR: The Secrets of Love**

The love of God must take precedent over all other aspects of life. Idolatry is the sin of putting too much importance upon persons, activities or things. Crossdressers have two temptations. First, the masculine side may desire power. Second, the feminine side may desire full feminine expression, and sometimes the expression comes at the expense of the people who share their lives or religious convictions. When people are able to place more emphasis upon the love of God than upon power and personal expression, many problems will have solutions. Remember that people of genius are admired; people of wealth are envied; people of power are feared; but people of character are trusted. The feminine nature moves away from power, but it is equally important that the feminine persona does not become an obsession at the expense of loved ones and worship.

"Thou shalt have no other Gods before me."
(Exodus 20:3)

THE COUNTER FORCE

I believe there is a direct relationship between living a life which is free from these social wrongs and maintaining a good relationship with others and with self. When this is achieved the crossdresser can move forward to a greater gift. In a conversation with Melanie recently she described such a spiritual awakening. The revelation had begun on a retreat in which a number of persons from the gender community experienced a marvelous interface with each other, with their own personal value, and the awesome power of a higher being. Melanie came home with the conviction that she held a rare and wonderful gift; she believed herself to be gender gifted. To Melanie the "gift" has opened the doorway for a deeper spirituality.

Melanie explained it this way. *"To gain insight into myself and a higher power that supersedes myself it is necessary for me to relinquish the control of my life. I am then able to listen to and hear the voice of the higher power. Before I emerged as a crossdresser three years ago, I was never able to do this. Relinquishing control is almost impossible for most males, because power is vital to the nature of masculinity. It is femininity which releases the more gentle side of me and makes me open to the guidance. I have called this awareness my personal JOURNEY TO SPIRITUALITY."*

It seems ironic that the world has provided accolades for the musically gifted but SHUNS OR EVEN FEARS THE GENDER GIFTED. The name, Beethoven, is etched upon musical history even as the musical compositions from this great musician linger in our hearts. Special schools are operated for gifted children, and these educational institutions become the catalyst for creativity and intellectual growth. Theaters, television and the motion picture industry regularly honor the gifted in their field. Where is the honor for the gender community? I believe crossdressers are the gender gifted; that rare and wonderful group of people who have touched the total of human life, both masculine and feminine. They have the power to enrich their own lives and the lives of others.

Vanessa has seen the potential of the community and writes about it in her book **THE CROSS AND THE CROSSDRESSER**. *"God has gifted certain individuals with the desire to experience unique aspects of life's infinite variety from a different perspective from that which our culture's norms permit. I refer to this as a 'gift' because I feel it is bestowed upon these persons as a mechanism for them to better understand themselves, other people, and the nature of God."*

THE MEANING OF GENDER GIFTED

The word "gifted" literally means, *"Having natural ability or special talents."* Thus, gender gifted people could be defined as those persons who have a special range of gender expression and the unique ability to experience the feelings and emotions which traditionally are associated with the opposite sex. The gender gifted individuals are able to break away from role expectations, experience the total of human life, and move across the lines which usually separate men from women.

While society has relaxed some of the lines, to a large degree we still live in a male-dominated society. Gender gifted people have the ability to draw upon the dominance needed to make power decisions and the sensitivity to foster effectiveness. It is the feminine side that gives people an ability to direct and handle people in a more compassionate manner. To be gender gifted means having the sensitivity to tune into human nature with an appreciation for people while demonstrating the qualities of masculine strength. Our founding fathers were right when they wrote, *"All men are created equal."* The challenge of being gender gifted is to "outgrow" the equality and move into the "gift".

INTEGRATING THE TOTAL PERSONALITY

Balance and integration will be vital in the quest for the gender "gift." These qualities will follow an understanding of two key words. First, the word "organization" has a masculine connotation, since men tend to "make things work." The word "organism" has a feminine connotation, since this word is synonymous with life. Women, as real or potential mothers, possess the creativity which fosters the growth process. They nurture life and allow growth to follow its own mysterious law of becoming. Gender gifted people who draw upon all aspects of their nature can organize and provide life for the organization, family, or individual life.

Care must be taken to draw out the best gender qualities and forsake the negative ones. The organizational expertise should be allowed to flourish, but it must be tempered with the life blood which comes with feminine expression. As Emerson wrote, *"It is one of the most beautiful compensations of life that no man can sincerely try to help another without helping himself."*

As the search continues for the balance and integration there must always be an effort to prevent the wide pendulum swings which could be described as a neurotic glorification of either the masculine or the feminine personality. Some crossdressers, such as Donna, no longer need fancy clothing to express their femininity. On the other hand there is no longer the need for a strong glorification of the masculine which may result in a devaluation of femininity and a distorted emphasis upon power. Men tend to gain power by taking power away from others. The feminine nature would desire to gain reputation and a position of leadership by sharing and nurturing others. People who let their femininity flourish have power which is available to others.

On the other end of the continuum are those who are fearful of any sign of feminine nature. Such fear causes a tendency to denounce feminine expression. The cultural attitude which perceives women to be second class citizens fuels the distrust of crossdressers. Some people ask, *"Why would anyone want to imitate femininity?"*

THE SEXUAL DEVIANT

Strong contempt does not arise from ideology, but arises from an innate need to avoid guilt and anxiety. Many men have an uneasy truce between the mind and the body, a truce implanted by society. For most religious people, one of the greatest difficulties in accepting crossdressers has come when the community is perceived to be sexually deviant. The misunderstanding occurs because people believe sex and gender are the same. Before the label of "deviant" can be put to rest there must be some clarity. In the most simple explanation Virginia Prince has said, *"Gender is between the ears while sex is between the legs."* Or to say the same thing another way, sex is biological while gender is behavioral.

From the moment of birth our bodies identify us as either male or female. Almost immediately a set of behaviors are assigned to us, and these behaviors are expected to flourish in a line which is parallel to the birth sex. Thus, many people perceive gender to be a set of social expectations. Perhaps even as small children we had preferences that were not in line with gender expectations, but most of us have moved through life doing what we are "supposed" to do. Kaplan said this in a rather humorous way. *"I like chocolate ice cream; but when I go fishing, I use worms because fish like worms."* We bend our form to agree with the preferences of others. Then we file those imposed preferences in our minds until they become perceived to be a factual dictate. Michael McGriff, M.D., sees flexibility as one answer: *"Blessed are the flexible, for they shall not be bent out of shape."*

Traditionally, men are supposed to act, think and move like men, and any hint of the feminine is feared and soon becomes a catalyst for guilt and remorse.

In recent years some diversion from "normal" gender expectations have met with social acceptance. An example would be the movie, "Tootsie". Marjorie Garber believes this public acceptance came because gender itself was a subject for analysis. According to Garber, *" The movie was not threatening, and it was mainstream. In the movie Dorothy successfully 'passes' and gains both the secret pleasures and the effect."*

As the lines between the genders become less distinct the word "deviant" will be less appropriate as a description of the gender community.

UNCOVERING SOME MYTHS

Margaret Mead also described the roles assumed by men and women as dependent upon ideas implanted at an early age. But the problem with experiential learning, according to Doug Lawson, is that you never graduate. The outcomes of cultural and social constellations continue to evolve. This evolution has uncovered many myths. The fact that sex and gender should and will match is a myth, and the fact that ideas about sex and gender are set and established is also a myth. Erikson concluded after extensive observation that psychological trends are determined primarily biologically and secondarily by the expectation of a social role. There are many shades of gray and degrees of variance between the two. Perhaps Freud was not aware of the gray areas when he wrote, *"When you meet a human being, the first distinction you make is 'male or female', and you are accustomed to making the distinction with unhesitating certainty."*

THE KEY TO UNITY

The duality of the sexes could be perceived as an antithesis at the very heart of creation, an antithesis crying for synthesis. Gender gifted individuals have found the key to restitution and unity. In Taoism the feminine Yin is calm and receptive. In George Bernard Shaw's MAN AND SUPERMAN, Don Juan said, *"I came to believe that in her voice was all the music of the song, in her face all the beauty of the painting, and in her soul all the emotion of the poem."*

The masculine Yang, on the other hand, is portrayed in literature as active and generative. But there is a higher power available when individuals draw from the best of both genders. In psychological terms, this is the path toward "self-actualization," reaching the potential for doing the best that can be achieved within the range of options. Gender gifted individuals believe in "living" the total of humanity. One person with a belief is greater than ninety nine with only an interest.

NICE GUYS AND GALS FINISH FIRST

Perhaps it is time to challenge the Leo Durocher concept that "nice guys finish last." While Leo was talking about the New York Giants, this could surely extend to include the tendency to subdue the more gentle side of the personality. Crossdressers are rare individuals who should make a deliberate choice to combine the best of all genders. According to Charles Schultz, *"Life is like a ten-speed. Most of us have gears we never use."* Try on some new gears; you might like them.

A popular television show asks the question, *"How do they do that?"* Many have asked this question about those individuals that are truly gender gifted, including the people who possess the gift. Stoller quotes a question from a transvestite, *"When I am like a female, dressed in her clothes and appearing to be like her, am I still a male?"* Stoller answers, *"Yes, you are still intact. You are a male, no matter how many feminine clothes you put on."*

Most gender gifted individuals really do not understand how they are able to be in touch with the truth of Stoller's quote yet experience a full range of emotional expression. James Thurber may have been correct when he said, *"It is better to know some of the questions, than all of the answers."* Our myriad of questions will fade into the realization of self-actualization and a vision described by William Wordsworth.

"He beheld a vision, and adored the thing he saw. Arabian fiction never filled the world with the wonders that were wrought for him."

101

IF WE HAD OUR "DRUTHERS"

Cartoonist Al Capp created a dish of food called "DRUTHERS". No one could pass up this commendable delicacy, because most folks would "druther" eat it than anything else. Most of us have never seen it, tasted it, or enjoyed it. So it is the same with human nature. Most people do not have the gift of total gender expression, but for those persons with the gift there remains one burning question. Wouldn't you "druther" be the most complete human being possible? Many of us feel that circumstances prevent us from living life to the fullest; but according to Hugh Downs, "*A happy person is not a person in a certain set of circumstances, but rather a person with a certain set of attitudes.*"

FINDING CONGRUENCE

"*It is never too late to be what you might have been.*"
George Elliot

Frequently people ask, "*How do I find a relationship between crossdressing and religion? How do we reach our potential?*" The answer to these questions can be found, in part, with a definition of religion provided by Dr. Jaye Reviere.

"*Philosophically, religion systematically deals with issues of morality, quality of life, and human values. It works to establish systems and procedures in which people can abide. Thus, at its core, religion is concerned with a fundamental life philosophy and a basis for life. In the United States of America, we experience a religious environment which is highly diverse yet undergirded by some fundamental principles."*

In his book, DEUTERONOMY, David Payne focuses on the internal as opposed to the external. Payne feels the faith we have experienced in our hearts should be evident to the persons who observe our lives. To extend the idea about the external manifestation of our faith a bit further, I believe we are all challenged to be the most loving, compassionate people possible. As a group I feel crossdressers try very hard to show this kind of feeling for others. Perhaps the greatest wrong could be the failure to do this. For example, crossdressers must consider the feelings and needs of those they love as much as possible.

I believe crossdressers are loved by God and should not feel guilty for the expression of their true identity. It behooves us to look beyond the confusion and despair and into the very nature of a God whose love knows no boundaries. We do not serve a God who would mold a person one way and later condemn him for inner expression of what was created.

The God I know exemplifies mercy and understanding rather than wrath. My God would not want crossdressers to experience agony as they attempt to coexist within their true nature. He would reach out compassionately to them.

As a wife, I believe God wants me to be aware of the pain of rejection which has been felt by thousands of crossdressers, purge after purge and tear after tear. If I see a need for acceptance, how can I turn away? My faith, though it was based upon very conservative traditional religious values, is big enough to accept and love all aspects of my husband's personality and the personalities of others like him, even those who do not fit the traditional "mold."

In the book written by Vanessa S., **THE CROSS AND THE CROSSDRESSER**, the author, a crossdresser, describes the obligation each of us has to ourselves. "*As unique and autonomous individuals we are not responsible for what others may say or think, even though we may care very deeply about those words or thoughts. It is up to each of us to determine and live out the truth as best we can discern it. I must submit to God's design and actively love persons made in the image of God.*"

Jesus was painfully aware of not being understood, and was himself rebuked by religious leaders who quoted the law. Christ always pointed to the greater law which is grace and love. So it is important to look inward. Love must be the point of focus, rather than what the Bible calls external "trappings."

"*God chose what is foolish in the world to shame the wise. God chose what is weak in the world to show the strong.*"
*(*I Corinthians 1: 27)

Will crossdressers suffer because of who they are? I believe they may, but there is assurance in faith and in the Holy Bible which says, "*More than that, we will rejoice in our sufferings, knowing that suffering produces endurance, and endurance produces character, and character produces hope, and hope does not disappoint us, because God's love has poured into our hearts.*" (Romans 5: 3-5)

Living a God-like life is never easy. Adding the complexity of being a part of a misunderstood minority makes life even more difficult. But crossdressers must come to the point of understanding the intrinsic nature of who they are, and make the most of what can be a rewarding life based upon principles of right or wrong, rather than upon customs or outdated law.

Sally has been guided by truth and integrity.

Sheila Kirk has inspired the term "gender gifted".

EPILOGUE

By: Jane Ellen Fairfax, M.D.

Crossdressing is a life-wrenching experience for both the crossdresser and his loved ones. Making peace with it is, in the words of the Mother Abbess, *"a dream that will need all the love you can give, Every day of your life, for as long as you live"*.

Because society sees everything in one-dimensional black and white, it does not perceive the breadth and depth that makes the crossdresser a truly gifted person. Crossdressers are blessed with stacks of masculine and feminine lumber, from which they can build their personalities. The potential for personal development is enormous! Social attitudes have wronged crossdressers and those who love them. Whether crossdressers can fulfill their potential as people depends on whether they choose to wallow in that sense of wrong or rise about it. Dr. Rudd offers brilliant insights by which crossdressers can transcend selfishness and fulfill their potentials in personal development and relationship-building.

Not all crossdressers perceive their femininity as a gift. Demeaned by social expectations, they become mired in a morass of guilt and fear. Eventually, frustration can lead to an explosion of selfishness. This need not happen. In one of his books Dr. James Herriot told the story of a deeply depressed man whose dog was slowly going blind. Overwhelmed by gloom and self-hate, the man did not want to live. But he loved his dog, and knew he must provide for him. Because he fulfilled the responsibility of love for his dog, he, as well as the dog, rose above the problem.

There is, for crossdressers, a similar way out of self-rejection. We can concentrate on using our gender gift to fulfill our responsibilities to those we love, to our fellow creatures, and to God. Happiness starts for us, and those we love, when we learn to accept ourselves. Reading the literature will reinforce our sense of worth as human beings. Motivated by a sense of responsibility, and buoyed by knowledge, we are ready to share our full selves with our loved ones. Out reaches the extended hand of love.

For the loved one exposure to crossdressing can be frightening. Dr. Rudd's balanced presentation vividly delineates the wide range of responses to being told about crossdressing. Crossdressers and their loved ones face strikingly similar issues - isolation, social condemnation, fear for job, and even self-image. Likewise, strategies for coping are strikingly similar. Self-acceptance and removal of "fault" come first, reinforced by knowledge gleaned from the literature. Both crossdressers and their families and friends must remove the blinders of self-pity, so that they can see and love the beauty of God's creatures. As the crossdresser and his loved ones reach out, their hands meet in a close bond. By sharing deeply and following the steps of intimacy, the bond grows ever stronger.

In this book, Dr. Rudd has given us a golden key to happiness. All we have to do is use it to open the door, and walk through!

Dr. Jane Ellen Fairfax is chair of the Tri-Ess National
Board of Directors.

RESOURCES

AEGIS
P.O. Box 33724
Decatur, Georgia 30033

Creative Design Services
P.O. Box 61263
King of Prussia, Pennsylvania 19406

Cross-Talk
P.O. Box 944
Woodland Hills, California 91365

Grace and Lace Newsletter
P.O. Box 31253
Jacksonville, Mississippi 39286-1253

International Foundation of Gender Education
P.O. Box 367
Wayland, Massachusetts 01778

Outreach Institute
126 Western Ave., Suite 246
Augusta, Maine 04330

Tri-Ess
P.O. Box 194
Tulare, California 93275

Tri-Ess Department of Wives' and Partners' Support
Linda Peacock
P.O. Box 24031
Little Rock, Arkansas 72221

BIBLIOGRAPHY

Allen, M. Transformations: Crossdressers and Those Who Love Them. New York: E. P. Dutton. 1988.

Brierley, H. Transvestism: Illness, Perversion, Choice. New York: Pergamon. 1979.

Bullough, V. and Bullough,B. Crossdressing, Sex, and Gender. Philadelphia, PA. University of Pennsylvania Press. 1993.

Bush, Barbara. Barbara Bush: A Memoire. New York: Charles Scribner's Sons. 1994.

Docter, Richard F. Transvestites and Transsexuals: Toward a Theory of Cross-Gender Behavior. New York. Plenum Press. 1988.

Duncan, Barry. Overcoming Relationship Impasses. New York. Insight Books. 1993.

Freud, Sigmund. In New Lectures On Psycho-Analysis. London: The Hogart Press. 1993.

Garber, Marjorie. Vested Interests. London: Routledge, Chapman, and Hall. 1992.

Helms, K. Religion And The Cross Gender Behavior: Wellspring Of Hope Or Swamp Of Despair, a paper presented to the First International Congress on Gender, Crossdressing, and Sex Issues, Los Angeles, February, 1995.

Keys, Ken. The Power of Unconditional Love. Coos Bay, Oregon. Love Line Press. 1990.

Miller, Jeff. Testosterone Out of Kilter? Try a Filter. Houston Chronicle, October 9, 1994. Section 5c.

Mullen, Paul. Jealousy, An Independent Study. Melbourne: Monash University. 1994.

Peacock, L. "Woman Who Are You?" CROSS-TALK. Vol. 62, p. 10.

Pietropinto, A.. and Simenauer, J. Beyond the Male Myth. New York. Times Books. 1977.

Prince, V. The Transvestite and His Wife. Los Angeles. Chevalier Publications. 1973.

Prince, V. Understanding Cross Dressing. Los Angeles. Chevalier Publications. 1976.

Roberts, JoAnn. Coping With Crossdressing. King of Prussia, Pennsylvania. Creative Design Services. 1993.

Rudd, Peggy. Crossdressing With Dignity. Katy, Texas. PM Publishers. 1991.

Rudd, Peggy. Love Calendar. Katy, Texas. PM Publishers. 1994.

Rudd, Peggy. My Husband Wears My Clothes. Katy, Texas. PM Publishers. 1989.

Stuart, Kim. The Uninvited Dilemma. Portland, Oregon. Metamorphosis Press. 1983.

Other books by Peggy J. Rudd, Ed.D.

USE THIS CONVENIENT ORDER FORM TO ORDER ADDITIONAL BOOKS

Name _____

Address _____

City _____

State _____ Zip Code _____

I would like to order:

_____ CROSSDRESSERS: AND THOSE WHO SHARE
         THEIR LIVES @ $14.95
_____ MY HUSBAND WEARS MY CLOTHES
         @ $12.95
_____ CROSSDRESSING WITH DIGNITY
         @ $12.95
_____ LOVE CALENDAR: The Secrets of Love
         @ $9.95
_____ All four books $39.00

_____ Sub-total

_____ Postage & Handling

_____ Texas residents add 8% sales tax

_____ Total

FOR DOMESTIC ORDERS ADD 15% FOR P/H
FOR INTERNATIONAL ORDERS ADD 25% FOR P/H

Please send order form and check or money order to:

PM Publishers
PO Box 5304
Katy, TX 77491-5304
Fax (713) 347-8747

Please note: this form may be duplicated.